let's cook
one pot

Sarah
Green

p

Contents

Country Chicken Hot-Pot

There are many regional versions of hot-pot, all using fresh, local ingredients. Now there are an endless variety of ingredients available all year, perfect for traditional one-pot cooking.

Serves 4

INGREDIENTS

4 chicken quarters
6 medium potatoes, cut
   into 5 mm/$^{1}/_{4}$ inch slices
2 sprigs thyme
2 sprigs rosemary
2 bay leaves

200 g/7 oz/1 cup rindless, smoked
   streaky bacon, diced
1 large onion, chopped finely
200 g/7 oz/1 cup sliced carrots
150 ml/$^{1}/_{4}$ pint/$^{2}/_{3}$ cup stout
25 g/1 oz/2 tbsp melted butter

salt and pepper

1 Remove the skin from the chicken quarters, if preferred.

2 Arrange a layer of potato slices in the bottom of a wide casserole. Season with salt and pepper, then add the thyme, rosemary and bay leaves.

3 Top with the chicken quarters, then sprinkle with the diced bacon, onion and carrots. Season well and arrange the remaining potato slices on top, overlapping slightly.

4 Pour over the stout, brush the potatoes with the melted butter and cover with a lid.

5 Bake in a preheated oven, 150°C/300°F/Gas Mark 2, for about 2 hours, uncovering for the last 30 minutes to allow the potatoes to brown. Serve hot.

COOK'S TIP

Serve the hot-pot with dumplings for a truly hearty meal.

VARIATION

This dish is also delicious with stewing lamb, cut into chunks. You can add different vegetables depending on what is in season – try leeks and swedes for a slightly sweeter flavour.

Bourguignonne of Chicken

A recipe based on a classic French dish. Use a good quality wine when making this casserole.

Serves 4–6

INGREDIENTS

4 tbsp sunflower oil
900 g/1³/₄ lb chicken meat, diced
250 g/9 oz/3 cups button
   mushrooms
125 g/4¹/₂ oz/²/₃ cup rindless,
   smoked bacon, diced
16 shallots

2 garlic cloves, crushed
1 tbsp plain (all-purpose) flour
150 ml/¹/₄ pint/²/₃ cup white
   Burgundy wine
150 ml/¹/₄ pint/²/₃ cup chicken stock

1 bouquet garni (1 bay leaf, sprig
   thyme, stick of celery, parsley and
   sage tied with string)
salt and pepper
deep-fried croûtons and a selection
   of cooked vegetables, to serve

1 Heat the sunflower oil in an ovenproof casserole and brown the chicken all over. Remove from the casserole with a slotted spoon.

2 Add the mushrooms, bacon, shallots and garlic to the casserole and cook for 4 minutes.

3 Return the chicken to the casserole and sprinkle with flour. Cook for a further 2 minutes, stirring.

4 Add the Burgundy wine and chicken stock to the casserole and stir until boiling. Add the bouquet garni and season well with salt and pepper.

5 Cover the casserole and bake in the centre of a preheated oven, 150°C/300°F/Gas Mark 2, for 1½ hours. Remove the bouquet garni.

6 Deep fry some heart-shaped croûtons (about 8 large ones) in beef dripping(s) and serve with the bourguignonne.

COOK'S TIP

A good quality red wine can be used instead of the white wine, to produce a rich, glossy red sauce.

Brittany Chicken Casserole

A hearty, one-dish meal that would make a substantial lunch or supper. As it requires a long cooking time, make double quantities and freeze half to eat later.

Serves 6

INGREDIENTS

500 g/1 lb 2 oz/2^1/2 cups beans,
   such as flageolets,
   soaked overnight and drained
25 g/1 oz/2 tbsp butter
2 tbsp olive oil
3 rindless bacon slices, chopped

900 g/1^3/4 lb chicken pieces
1 tbsp plain (all-purpose) flour
300 ml/^{1}/2 pint/1^1/4 cups cider
150 ml/^{1}/4 pint/^{2}/3 cup chicken stock
14 shallots
2 tbsp honey, warmed

250 g/8 oz ready-cooked beetroot
salt and pepper

1 Cook the beans in salted boiling water for about 25 minutes.

2 Heat the butter and olive oil in a flameproof casserole, add the bacon and chicken and cook for 5 minutes.

3 Sprinkle with the flour then add the cider and chicken stock, stirring constantly to avoid lumps forming. Season with salt and pepper to taste and bring to the boil.

4 Add the beans then cover the casserole tightly with a lid or cooking foil and bake in the centre of a preheated oven, 160°C/325°F/ Gas Mark 3, for 2 hours.

5 About 15 minutes before the end of cooking time, remove the lid or cooking foil from the casserole.

6 In a frying pan (skillet), gently cook the shallots and honey together for 5 minutes, turning the shallots frequently.

7 Add the shallots and cooked beetroot to the casserole and leave to finish cooking in the oven for the last 15 minutes.

COOK'S TIP

To save time, use canned flageolet beans instead of dried. Drain and rinse before adding to the chicken.

Scotch Broth

*This traditional winter soup is full of goodness,
with lots of tasty golden vegetables along with tender barley and lamb.*

Serves 4-6

INGREDIENTS

60 g/2 oz/⅓ cup pearl barley
300 g/10½ oz lean boneless lamb,
    such as shoulder or neck fillet,
    trimmed of fat and cut into 1 cm/
    ½ inch cubes
700 ml/1¼ pints/3 cups water
1 onion, finely chopped

2 garlic cloves, finely chopped or
    crushed
1 litre/1¾ pints/4 cups chicken or
    meat stock
1 large leek, quartered lengthways
    and sliced
2 large carrots, finely diced

1 parsnip, finely diced
125 g/4½ oz peeled swede (rutabaga),
    diced
2 tbsp chopped fresh parsley
salt and pepper
1 bay leaf

1 Rinse the barley under cold running water. Put in a saucepan and cover generously with water. Bring to the boil and boil for 3 minutes, skimming off the foam from the surface. Set aside, covered, in the saucepan.

2 Put the lamb in a large saucepan with the water and bring to the boil. Skim off the foam that rises to the surface.

3 Stir in the garlic, stock, onion and bay leaf. Reduce the heat and boil very gently, partially covered, for 15 minutes.

4 Drain the barley and add to the soup. Add the leek, carrots, parsnip and swede (rutabaga). Continue simmering for about 1 hour, or until the lamb and vegetables are tender, stirring occasionally.

5 Taste and adjust the seasoning. Stir in the parsley and ladle into warm bowls to serve.

COOK'S TIP

This soup is lean when the lamb is trimmed. By making it beforehand, you can remove any hardened fat before reheating.

Spanish Paella

*This classic recipe gets its name from the wide metal pan
traditionally used for cooking the dish – a paellera.*

Serves 4

INGREDIENTS

120 ml/4 fl oz/$\frac{1}{2}$ cup olive oil

1.5 kg/3 lb 5 oz chicken, cut into
   8 pieces

350 g/12 oz chorizo sausage, cut into
   1 cm/$\frac{1}{2}$ inch pieces

115 g/4 oz cured ham, chopped

2 onions, finely chopped

2 red (bell) peppers, cored, deseeded
   and cut into 2.5 cm/1 inch pieces

4–6 garlic cloves

750 g/1 lb 10 oz/$3\frac{3}{4}$ cups short-grain
   Spanish rice or Italian arborio rice

2 bay leaves

1 tsp dried thyme

1 tsp saffron threads, lightly crushed

225 ml/8 fl oz/1 cup dry white wine

1.5 litres/$2\frac{3}{4}$ pints/$6\frac{1}{4}$ cups chicken
   stock

115 g/4 oz fresh shelled or defrosted
   frozen peas

450 g/1 lb medium uncooked prawns
   (shrimp)

8 raw King prawns (shrimp), in shells

16 clams, very well scrubbed

16 mussels, very well scrubbed

salt and pepper

4 tbsp chopped fresh flat-leaf parsley

1 Heat half the oil in a 46 cm/
18 inch paella pan or deep,
wide frying pan (skillet) over a
medium-high heat. Add the
chicken and fry gently, turning,
until golden brown. Remove from
the pan and set aside.

2 Add the chorizo and ham to
the pan and cook for about 7
minutes, stirring occasionally, until
crisp. Remove and set aside.

3 Stir the onions into the pan
and cook for about 3 minutes
until soft. Add the (bell) peppers
and garlic and cook until beginning
to soften; remove and set aside.

4 Add the remaining oil to the
pan and stir in the rice until
well coated. Add the bay leaves,
thyme and saffron and stir well.
Pour in the wine, bubble, then
pour in the stock, stirring well and

scraping the bottom of the pan.
Bring to the boil, stirring often.

5 Stir in the cooked vegetables.
Add the chorizo, ham and
chicken and gently bury in the rice.
Reduce the heat and cook for 10
minutes, stirring occasionally.

6 Add the peas and prawns
(shrimp) and cook for a
further 5 minutes. Push the clams
and mussels into the rice. Cover
and cook over a very low heat for
about 5 minutes until the rice is
tender and the shellfish open.
Discard any unopened clams or
mussels. Season to taste.

7 Remove from heat, and stand,
covered, for about 5 minutes.
Sprinkle with parsley and serve.

Pasta & Bean Casserole

*A satisfying winter dish, pasta and bean casserole with a
crunchy topping is a slow-cooked, one-pot meal.*

Serves 6

INGREDIENTS

225 g/8 oz/1^1/$_4$ cups dried haricot
(navy) beans, soaked overnight
and drained
225 g/8 oz dried penne
6 tbsp olive oil
850 ml/1^1/$_2$ pints /3^1/$_2$ cups
vegetable stock
2 large onions, sliced

2 garlic cloves, chopped
2 bay leaves
1 tsp dried oregano
1 tsp dried thyme
5 tbsp red wine
2 tbsp tomato purée (paste)
2 celery sticks (stalks), sliced
1 fennel bulb, sliced

115 g/4 oz/1^5/$_8$ cups sliced
mushrooms
250 g/8 oz tomatoes, sliced
1 tsp dark muscovado sugar
4 tbsp dry white breadcrumbs
salt and pepper
salad leaves (greens) and crusty
bread, to serve

1 Put the haricot (navy) beans
in a large saucepan and add
sufficient cold water to cover.
Bring to the boil and continue to
boil vigorously for 20 minutes.
Drain, set aside and keep warm.

2 Bring a large saucepan of
lightly salted water to the
boil. Add the penne and 1 tbsp of
the olive oil and cook for about 3
minutes. Drain the pasta, set aside
and keep warm.

3 Put the beans in a large,
flameproof casserole. Add the
vegetable stock and stir in the
remaining olive oil, the onions,
garlic, bay leaves, oregano, thyme,
wine and tomato purée (paste).
Bring to the boil, then cover and
cook in a preheated oven at
180°C/350°F/Gas 4 for 2 hours.

4 Add the penne, celery, fennel,
mushrooms and tomatoes to
the casserole and season to taste

with salt and pepper. Stir in the
muscovado sugar and sprinkle
over the breadcrumbs. Cover the
dish and cook in the oven for
1 further hour.

5 Serve hot with salad leaves
(greens) and crusty bread.

Potato & Mushroom Bake

Use any mixture of mushrooms to hand for this creamy layered bake.
It can be served straight from the dish in which it is cooked.

Serves 4

INGREDIENTS

25 g/1 oz butter
450 g/1 lb waxy potatoes, thinly
  sliced
150 g/5 oz mixed mushrooms, sliced

1 tbsp chopped fresh rosemary
4 tbsp chopped fresh chives
2 garlic cloves, crushed

150 ml/$\frac{1}{4}$ pint/$\frac{2}{3}$ cup double
  (heavy) cream
salt and pepper
fresh chives, to garnish

1 Grease a shallow round ovenproof dish with butter.

2 Parboil the sliced potatoes in a saucepan of boiling water for 10 minutes. Drain well. Layer a quarter of the potatoes in the base of the dish.

3 Arrange a quarter of the mushrooms on top of the potatoes and sprinkle with a quarter of the rosemary, chives and garlic.

4 Continue layering in the same order, finishing with a layer of potatoes on top.

5 Pour the cream over the top of the potatoes. Season well.

6 Cook in a preheated oven, 190°C/375°F/Gas Mark 5, for 45 minutes or until the bake is golden brown.

7 Garnish with fresh chives and serve at once.

COOK'S TIP

For a special occasion, the bake may be made in a lined cake tin (pan) and turned out to serve.

VARIATION

Use 50 g/2 oz re-hydrated dried mushrooms instead of the fresh mixed mushrooms, for a really intense flavour.

Potato, Beef & Peanut Pot

The spicy peanut sauce in this recipe will complement almost any meat; although beef is used here, the dish is just as delicious made with chicken or pork.

Serves 4

INGREDIENTS

1 tbsp vegetable oil
60 g/2 oz/^{1}/$_4$ cup butter
450 g/1 lb lean beef steak, cut into thin strips
1 onion, halved and sliced
2 garlic cloves, crushed

2 large waxy potatoes, cubed
^{1}/$_2$ tsp paprika
4 tbsp crunchy peanut butter
600 ml/1 pint/2^1/$_2$ cups beef stock
25 g/1 oz unsalted peanuts
2 tsp light soy sauce

50 g/1^3/$_4$ oz sugar snap peas
1 red (bell) pepper, cut into strips
parsley sprigs, to garnish (optional)

1 Heat the oil and butter in a flameproof casserole dish.

2 Add the beef strips and fry them gently for 3-4 minutes, stirring and turning the meat until it is sealed on all sides.

3 Add the onion and garlic and cook for a further 2 minutes, stirring constantly.

4 Add the potato cubes and cook for 3-4 minutes or until they begin to brown slightly.

5 Stir in the paprika and peanut butter, then gradually blend in the beef stock. Bring the mixture to the boil, stirring frequently.

6 Finally, add the peanuts, soy sauce, sugar snap peas and red (bell) pepper.

7 Cover and cook over a low heat for 45 minutes or until the beef is cooked through.

8 Garnish the dish with parsley sprigs, if wished, and serve.

COOK'S TIP

Serve this dish with plain boiled rice or noodles, if you wish.

VARIATION

Add a chopped green chilli to the sauce for extra spice, if you prefer.

Creamy Chicken & Potato Casserole

Small new potatoes are ideal for this recipe as they can be cooked whole. If larger potatoes are used, cut them in half or into chunks before adding them to the casserole.

Serves 4

INGREDIENTS

2 tbsp vegetable oil
60 g/2 oz/$^1/_4$ cup butter
4 chicken portions, about 225 g/8 oz each
2 leeks, sliced
1 garlic clove, crushed
4 tbsp plain (all-purpose) flour

900 ml/1$^1/_2$ pints/3$^3/_4$ cups chicken stock
300 ml/$^1/_2$ pint/1$^1/_4$ cups dry white wine
125 g/4$^1/_2$ oz baby carrots, halved lengthways

125 g/4$^1/_2$ oz baby sweetcorn cobs (baby corn), halved lengthways
450 g/1 lb small new potatoes
1 bouquet garni
150 ml/$^1/_4$ pint/$^2/_3$ cup double (heavy) cream
salt and pepper

1 Heat the oil in a large frying pan (skillet). Cook the chicken for 10 minutes, turning until browned all over. Transfer the chicken to a casserole dish using a perforated spoon.

2 Add the leek and garlic to the frying pan (skillet) and cook for 2-3 minutes, stirring. Stir in the flour and cook for a further 1 minute. Remove the frying pan (skillet) from the heat and stir in the stock and wine. Season well.

3 Return the pan to the heat and bring the mixture to the boil. Stir in the carrots, sweetcorn, potatoes and bouquet garni.

4 Transfer the mixture to the casserole dish. Cover and cook in a preheated oven, 180°C/350°F/Gas Mark 4, for about 1 hour.

5 Remove the casserole from the oven and stir in the cream. Return the casserole to the oven, uncovered, and cook for a further 15 minutes. Remove the bouquet garni and discard. Taste and adjust the seasoning, if necessary. Serve the casserole with plain rice or fresh vegetables, such as broccoli.

COOK'S TIP

Use turkey fillets instead of the chicken, if preferred, and vary the vegetables according to those you have to hand.

Chick-pea (Garbanzo Bean) & Vegetable Casserole

This hearty dish is best served with warm crusty bread to mop up the delicious juices.

Serves 4

INGREDIENTS

1 tbsp olive oil
1 red onion, halved and sliced
3 garlic cloves, crushed
225 g/8 oz spinach
1 fennel bulb, cut into eight
1 red (bell) pepper, cubed

1 tbsp plain (all-purpose) flour
450 ml/³/₄ pint/3³/₄ cups vegetable stock
85 ml/3 fl oz/6 tbsp dry white wine
400 g/14 oz can chick-peas (garbanzo beans), drained

1 bay leaf
1 tsp ground coriander
¹/₂ tsp paprika
salt and pepper
fennel fronds, to garnish

1 Heat the olive oil in a large flameproof casserole dish and sauté the onion and garlic for 1 minute, stirring. Add the spinach and cook for 4 minutes or until wilted.

2 Add the fennel and (bell) pepper and cook for 2 minutes, stirring.

3 Stir in the flour and cook for 1 minute.

4 Add the stock, wine, chick-peas (garbanzo beans), bay leaf, coriander and paprika, cover and cook for 30 minutes. Season to taste, garnish with fennel fronds and serve immediately.

VARIATION

Replace the coriander with nutmeg, if you prefer, as it works particularly well with spinach.

COOK'S TIP

Use other canned pulses or mixed beans instead of the chick-peas (garbanzo beans), if you prefer.

Roasted Seafood

*Vegetables become deliciously sweet and juicy when they are
roasted, and they go particularly well with fish and seafood.*

Serves 4

INGREDIENTS

600 g/1lb 5oz new potatoes
3 red onions, cut into wedges
2 courgettes (zucchini), sliced into
 chunks

8 garlic cloves, peeled
2 lemons, cut into wedges
4 sprigs rosemary
4 tbsp olive oil

350 g/12oz shell-on prawns (shrimp),
 preferably uncooked
2 small squid, chopped into rings
4 tomatoes, quartered

1 Scrub the potatoes to remove any excess dirt. Cut any large potatoes in half. Place the potatoes in a large roasting tin (pan), together with the onions, courgettes (zucchini), garlic, lemon and rosemary.

2 Pour over the oil and toss to coat all of the vegetables in the oil.

3 Cook in a preheated oven, at 200°C/400°F/Gas Mark 6, for about 40 minutes, turning occasionally, until the potatoes are tender.

4 Once the potatoes are tender, add the prawns (shrimp), squid and tomatoes, tossing to coat them in the oil, and roast for 10 minutes. All of the vegetables should be cooked through and slightly charred for full flavour.

5 Transfer to serving plates and serve hot.

COOK'S TIP

*Squid and octopus are great
favourites in Italy and all around
the Mediterranean.*

VARIATION

*Most vegetables are suitable for
roasting in the oven. Try adding
450 g/ 1 lb pumpkin, squash or
aubergine (eggplant), if you prefer.*

Baked Tomato Rice with Sausages

A great quick supper for the family,
this dish is incredibly simple to put together, yet is truly scrumptious!

Serves 4

INGREDIENTS

2 tbsp vegetable oil
1 onion, coarsely chopped
1 red (bell) pepper, cored, deseeded
  and chopped
2 garlic cloves, finely chopped
1/2 tsp dried thyme

300 g/10^1/$_2$ oz/1^1/$_2$ cups long-grain
  white rice
1 litre/1^3/$_4$ pints/4 cups light chicken
  or vegetable stock
225 g/8 oz can chopped tomatoes
1 bay leaf
2 tbsp shredded fresh basil

175 g/6 oz mature (sharp) Cheddar
  cheese, grated
2 tbsp chopped fresh chives
4 herby pork sausages, cooked and cut
  into 1 cm/^{1}/$_2$ inch pieces
2–3 tbsp freshly grated Parmesan
  cheese

1 Heat the oil in a large flame-proof casserole over medium heat. Add the onion and red (bell) pepper and cook for about 5 minutes, stirring frequently, until soft and lightly coloured. Stir in the garlic and thyme and cook for a further minute.

2 Add the rice and cook, stirring frequently, for about 2 minutes until the rice is well coated and translucent. Stir in the stock, tomatoes and bay leaf. Boil for 5 minutes until the stock is almost absorbed.

3 Stir in the basil, Cheddar cheese, chives and pork sausages and bake, covered, in a preheated oven at 180°C/350°F/Gas Mark 4 for about 25 minutes.

4 Sprinkle with the Parmesan cheese and return to the oven, uncovered, for 5 minutes until the top is golden. Serve hot from the casserole.

VARIATION

For a vegetarian version, replace the pork sausages with a 400 g/14 oz can of drained butter beans, kidney beans, or sweetcorn. Or try a mixture of sautéed mushrooms and courgettes (zucchini).

Chicken Jalfrezi

This is a quick and tasty way to use leftover roast chicken. The sauce can also be used for any cooked poultry, lamb or beef.

Serves 4

INGREDIENTS

1 tsp mustard oil
3 tbsp vegetable oil
1 large onion, chopped finely
3 garlic cloves, crushed
1 tbsp tomato purée (paste)
2 tomatoes, peeled and chopped
1 tsp ground turmeric

$^1/_2$ tsp cumin seeds, ground
$^1/_2$ tsp coriander seeds, ground
$^1/_2$ tsp chilli powder
$^1/_2$ tsp garam masala
1 tsp red wine vinegar
1 small red (bell) pepper, chopped

125 g/4 oz/1 cup frozen broad (fava) beans
500 g/1 lb cooked chicken breasts, cut into bite-sized pieces
salt
fresh coriander (cilantro) sprigs, to garnish

1 Heat the mustard oil in a large, frying pan (skillet) set over a high heat for about 1 minute until it begins to smoke. Add the vegetable oil, reduce the heat and then add the onion and the garlic. Fry the garlic and onion until they are golden.

2 Add the tomato purée (paste), chopped tomatoes, ground turmeric, cumin and coriander seeds, chilli powder, garam masala and red wine vinegar to the frying pan (skillet). Stir the mixture until fragrant.

3 Add the red (bell) pepper and broad (fava) beans and stir for 2 minutes until the (bell) pepper is softened. Stir in the chicken, and salt to taste. Leave to simmer gently for 6-8 minutes until the chicken is heated through and the beans are tender.

4 Serve garnished with coriander (cilantro) leaves.

COOK'S TIP

This dish is an ideal way of making use of leftover poultry – turkey, duck or quail. Any variety of beans works well, but vegetables are just as useful, especially root vegetables, courgettes (zucchini), potatoes or broccoli. Leafy vegetables will not be so successful.

Beef Cooked in Whole Spices

*This is a delicious way of cooking beef. The fragrant whole
spices perfectly complement the meat.*

Serves 4

INGREDIENTS

300 ml/^{1}/2 pint/1^1/4 cups oil
3 medium onions, chopped finely
2.5 cm/1 inch ginger root, shredded
4 cloves garlic, shredded
2 cinnamon sticks

3 whole green cardamoms
3 whole cloves
4 whole black peppercorns
6 dried red chillies
150 ml/5 fl oz/^{2}/3 cup yogurt

450 g/1 lb beef, with or without bone
3 green chillies, chopped
600 ml/1 pint/2^1/2 cups water
fresh coriander (cilantro) leaves

1 Heat the oil in a frying pan
(skillet) and fry the onion,
stirring, until golden brown.

2 Reduce the heat and add the
ginger, garlic, cinnamon sticks,
green cardamoms, cloves, black
peppercorns and red chillies to the
pan and stir-fry for 5 minutes.

3 In a bowl, whip the yogurt
with a fork. Add the yogurt to
the onions and stir to combine.

4 Add the meat and 2 of the
green chillies to the frying

pan (skillet) and stir-fry the
mixture for 5-7 minutes.

5 Gradually add the water to the
pan, stirring well. Cover the
pan and cook the beef and spice
mixture for 1 hour, stirring and
adding more water if necessary.

6 When thoroughly cooked
through, remove the pan
from the heat and transfer the beef
and spice mixture to a serving
dish. Garnish with the remaining
chopped green chilli and the fresh
coriander (cilantro) leaves.

VARIATION

*Substitute lamb for the beef in this
recipe, if you prefer.*

Hungarian Chicken Goulash

Goulash is traditionally made with beef, but this recipe successfully uses chicken instead.
To reduce fat, use a low-fat cream in place of the soured cream.

Serves 6

INGREDIENTS

900 g/1³/₄ lb chicken meat, diced
60 g/2 oz/¹/₂ cup flour, seasoned
   with 1 tsp paprika, salt and pepper
2 tbsp olive oil
25 g/1 oz/2 tbsp butter
1 onion, sliced
24 shallots, peeled

1 each red and green
   (bell) pepper, chopped
1 tbsp paprika
1 tsp rosemary, crushed
4 tbsp tomato purée (paste)
300 ml/¹/₂ pint/1¹/₄ cups
   chicken stock

150 ml/¹/₄ pint/²/₃ cup claret
400 g/14 oz can chopped tomatoes
150 ml/¹/₄ pint/²/₃ cup soured cream
1 tbsp chopped fresh parsley,
   to garnish
chunks of bread and a side salad,
   to serve

1 Toss the chicken in the seasoned flour until it is coated all over.

2 In a flameproof casserole, heat the oil and butter and fry the onion, shallots and (bell) peppers for 3 minutes.

3 Add the chicken and cook for a further 4 minutes.

4 Sprinkle with the paprika and rosemary.

5 Add the tomato purée (paste), chicken stock, claret and chopped tomatoes, cover and cook in the centre of a preheated oven, 160°C/325°F/Gas Mark 3, for 1½ hours.

6 Remove the casserole from the oven, allow it to stand for 4 minutes, then add the soured cream and garnish with parsley.

7 Serve with chunks of bread and a side salad.

VARIATION

Serve the goulash with buttered ribbon noodles instead of bread. For an authentic touch, try a Hungarian red wine instead of the claret.

Jamaican Hot Pot

A tasty way to make chicken joints go a long way, this hearty casserole, spiced with the warm, subtle flavour of ginger, is a good choice for a Halloween party.

Serves 4

INGREDIENTS

2 tsp sunflower oil
4 chicken drumsticks
4 chicken thighs
1 medium onion
750 g/1 lb 10 oz piece squash
  or pumpkin, diced
1 green (bell) pepper, sliced

2.5 cm/1 inch fresh ginger root,
  chopped finely
400 g/14 oz can chopped
  tomatoes
300 ml/^{1}/$_2$ pint/1^1/$_4$ cups
  chicken stock

60 g/2 oz/^{1}/$_4$ cup
  split lentils
garlic salt and cayenne pepper
350 g/12 oz can sweetcorn
  (corn-on-the-cob)
crusty bread, to serve

1 Heat the oil in a large flameproof casserole and fry the chicken joints until golden, turning frequently.

2 Using a sharp knife, peel and slice the onion, peel and dice the pumpkin or squash and deseed and slice the (bell) pepper.

3 Drain any excess fat from the pan and add the prepared onion, pumpkin and (bell) pepper. Gently fry for a few minutes until lightly browned. Add the chopped ginger, tomatoes, chicken stock and lentils. Season lightly with garlic salt and cayenne pepper.

4 Cover the casserole and place in a preheated oven, 190°C/375°F/Gas Mark 5, for about 1 hour, until the vegetables are tender and the chicken juices run clear when pierced with a skewer.

5 Add the drained corn and cook for a further 5 minutes. Season to taste and serve with crusty bread.

VARIATION

If you can't find fresh ginger root, add 1 teaspoon allspice for a warm, fragrant aroma.

VARIATION

If squash or pumpkin is not available, swede (rutabaga) makes a good substitute.

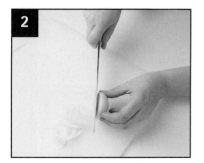

Chicken Madeira "French-style"

Madeira is a fortified wine which can be used in both sweet and savoury dishes.
Here it adds a rich, full flavour to the casserole.

Serves 8

INGREDIENTS

25 g/1 oz/2 tbsp butter
20 baby onions
250 g/9 oz/1^1/$_2$ cups carrots, sliced
250 g/9 oz/1^1/$_2$ cups bacon, chopped
250 g/9 oz/3 cups button
   mushrooms

1 chicken, weighing about 1.5 kg/
   3 lb 5 oz
425 ml/15 fl oz/1^7/$_8$ cups white wine
25 g/1 oz/^{1}/$_4$ cup seasoned flour
425ml/15 fl oz/1^7/$_8$ cups chicken
   stock

bouquet garni
150 ml/^{1}/$_4$ pint/^{2}/$_3$ cup Madeira wine
salt and pepper
mashed potato or pasta, to serve

1 Heat the butter in a large frying pan (skillet) and fry the onions, carrots, bacon and button mushrooms for 3 minutes, stirring frequently. Transfer to a large casserole dish.

2 Add the chicken to the frying pan (skillet) and brown all over. Transfer to the casserole dish with the vegetables and bacon.

3 Add the white wine and cook until the wine is nearly completely reduced.

4 Sprinkle with the seasoned flour, stirring to avoid lumps from forming.

5 Add the chicken stock, salt and pepper to taste and the bouquet garni. Cover and cook the casserole for 2 hours. About 30 minutes before the end of cooking time, add the Madeira wine and continue cooking uncovered.

6 Carve the chicken and serve with mashed potato or pasta.

COOK'S TIP

You can add any combination of herbs to this recipe – chervil is a popular herb in French cuisine, but add it at the end of cooking so that its delicate flavour is not lost. Other herbs which work well with chicken are parsley and tarragon.

Cantonese Garden Vegetable Stir-Fry

This dish tastes as fresh as it looks. Try to get hold of baby vegetables as they look and taste so much better in this dish.

Serves 4

INGREDIENTS

2 tbsp peanut oil
1 tsp Chinese five-spice powder
75 g/2^3/4 oz baby carrots, halved
2 celery sticks, sliced
2 baby leeks, sliced
50 g/1^3/4 oz mangetout (snow peas)

4 baby courgettes (zucchini), halved
   lengthwise
8 baby corn cobs
225 g/8 oz firm marinated
   tofu (bean curd), cubed
4 tbsp fresh orange juice

1 tbsp clear honey
celery leaves and orange zest, to
   garnish
cooked rice or noodles, to serve

---

1 Heat the oil in a preheated wok until almost smoking. Add the Chinese five-spice powder, carrots, celery, leeks, mangetout (snow peas), courgettes (zucchini) and corn cobs and stir-fry for 3–4 minutes.

2 Add the tofu (bean curd) and cook for a further 2 minutes, stirring.

3 Stir in the orange juice and honey, reduce the heat and cook for 1–2 minutes.

4 Transfer the stir-fry to a serving dish, garnish with celery leaves and orange zest and serve with rice or noodles.

COOK'S TIP

Chinese five-spice powder is a mixture of fennel, star anise, cinnamon bark, cloves and Szechuan pepper. It is very pungent so should be used sparingly. If kept in an airtight container, it will keep indefinitely.

VARIATION

Lemon juice would be just as delicious as the orange juice in this recipe, but use 3 tablespoons instead of 4 tablespoons.

Spicy Potato & Lemon Casserole

This is based on a Moroccan dish in which potatoes are spiced
with coriander (cilantro) and cumin and cooked in a lemon sauce.

Serves 4

INGREDIENTS

100 ml/3^1/2 fl oz/^{1}/2 cup olive oil
2 red onions, cut into eight
3 garlic cloves, crushed
2 tsp ground cumin
2 tsp ground coriander

pinch of cayenne pepper
1 carrot, thickly sliced
2 small turnips, quartered
1 courgette (zucchini), sliced
450 g/1 lb potatoes, thickly sliced

juice and rind of 2 large lemons
300 ml/^{1}/2 pint/1^1/4 cups vegetable
  stock
2 tbsp chopped coriander (cilantro)
salt and pepper

1 Heat the olive oil in a
flameproof casserole.

2 Add the red onion and sauté
for 3 minutes, stirring.

3 Add the garlic and cook for
30 seconds. Mix in the spices
and cook for 1 minute, stirring.

4 Add the carrot, turnips,
courgette (zucchini) and
potatoes and stir to coat in the oil.

5 Add the lemon juice and
rind, stock and salt and
pepper to taste, cover and cook
over a medium heat for 20–30
minutes, stirring occasionally.

6 Remove the lid, sprinkle in
the coriander (cilantro) and
stir well. Serve immediately.

COOK'S TIP

A selection of spices and herbs is
important for adding variety to your
cooking – add to your range each
time you try a new recipe.

COOK'S TIP

Check the vegetables whilst cooking
as they may begin to stick to the
pan. Add a little more boiling water
or stock if necessary.

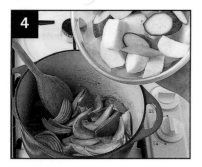

Potato, (Bell) Pepper & Mushroom Hash

This is a quick one-pan dish which is ideal for a quick snack. Packed with colour and flavour it is very versatile and you can add any other vegetable you have at hand.

Serves 4

INGREDIENTS

675 g/1$^{1}/_{2}$ lb potatoes, cubed
1 tbsp olive oil
2 garlic cloves, crushed
1 green (bell) pepper, cubed
1 yellow (bell) pepper, cubed

3 tomatoes, diced
75 g/2$^{3}/_{4}$ oz/1 cup button
  mushrooms, halved
1 tbsp vegetarian Worcester sauce
2 tbsp chopped basil

salt and pepper
fresh basil sprigs, to garnish
warm, crusty bread, to serve

1 Cook the potatoes in a saucepan of boiling salted water for 7–8 minutes. Drain well and reserve.

2 Heat the oil in a large, heavy-based frying pan (skillet) and cook the potatoes for 8–10 minutes, stirring until browned.

3 Add the garlic and (bell) peppers and cook for 2–3 minutes.

4 Stir in the tomatoes and mushrooms and cook, stirring, for 5–6 minutes.

5 Stir in the vegetarian Worcester sauce and basil and season well. Garnish and serve with crusty bread.

VARIATION

This dish can also be eaten cold as a salad.

COOK'S TIP

If cooking for vegetarians, make sure you use a brand of Worcestershire sauce that not contain anchovies.

Moroccan Fish Tagine

A tagine is a Moroccan cooking vessel consisting of an earthenware dish with a domed lid that has a steam hole in the top. However, this dish can be made quite successfully in an ordinary pan.

Serves 4

INGREDIENTS

2 tbsp olive oil
1 large onion, finely chopped
large pinch saffron strands
½ tsp ground cinnamon
1 tsp ground coriander
½ tsp ground cumin

½ tsp ground turmeric
200 g/7 oz can chopped tomatoes
300 ml/½ pint/1¼ cups fish stock
4 small red mullet cleaned, boned and
   heads and tails removed
50 g/1¾ oz pitted green olives

1 tbsp chopped preserved lemon
3 tbsp fresh chopped coriander
salt and pepper
couscous, to serve

---

1 Heat the olive oil in a large saucepan or flameproof casserole. Add the onion and cook gently for 10 minutes without colouring until softened. Add the saffron, cinnamon, coriander, cumin and turmeric and cook for a further 30 seconds, stirring.

2 Add the chopped tomatoes and fish stock and stir well. Bring to the boil, cover and simmer for 15 minutes. Uncover and simmer for a further 20–35 minutes until thickened.

3 Cut each red mullet in half then add the pieces to the pan, pushing them into the sauce. Simmer gently for a further 5–6 minutes until the fish is just cooked.

4 Carefully stir in the olives, preserved lemon and the chopped coriander. Season to taste and serve with couscous.

COOK'S TIP

Preserved lemons are simple to make yourself. Take enough lemons to completely fill a preserving jar and quarter them lengthways without cutting all the way through. Pack the lemons with 50 g/1¾ oz/ ¼ cup sea salt per lemon, adding any remaining salt to the jar. Add the juice of a further lemon and top up with water to cover. Leave for at least 1 month before using.

Squid Stew

This is a rich and flavourful stew of slowly cooked squid, in a sauce of tomatoes and red wine. The squid becomes very tender.

Serves 4

INGREDIENTS

750 g/1 lb 10 oz squid
3 tbsp olive oil
1 onion, chopped
3 garlic cloves, finely chopped

1 tsp fresh thyme leaves
400 g/14 oz can chopped tomatoes
150 ml/5 fl oz/²/₃ cup red wine
300 ml/½ pint/1¼ cups water

1 tbsp chopped fresh parsley
salt and pepper

1 To prepare whole squid, hold the body firmly and grasp the tentacles just inside the body. Pull firmly to remove the innards. Find the transparent 'backbone' and remove. Grasp the wings on the outside of the body and pull to remove the outer skin. Trim the tentacles just below the beak and reserve. Wash the body and tentacles under running water. Slice the body into rings. Drain well on paper towels.

2 Heat the oil in a large, flameproof casserole. Add the prepared squid and cook over a medium heat, stirring occasionally, until lightly browned.

3 Reduce the heat and add the onion, garlic and thyme. Cook a further 5 minutes until softened.

4 Stir in the tomatoes, red wine and water. Bring to the boil and cook to a preheated oven at 140°C/275°F/Gas Mark 1 for 2 hours. Stir in the parsley and season to taste.

VARIATIONS

This stew can be used as the basis for a more substantial fish stew. Before adding the parsley, add extra seafood such as scallops, pieces of fish fillet, large prawns (jumbo shrimp) or even cooked lobster. Return the stew to the boil and cook a further 2 minutes. Add the parsley and seasoning.

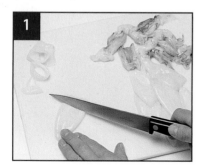

NOTE

Cup measurements in this book are for American cups. This book uses
imperial and metric measurements. Follow the same units of measurement
throughout; do not mix imperial and metric. All spoon measurements are
level; teaspoons are assumed to be 5 ml and tablespoons are assumed to be
15 ml. Unless otherwise stated, milk is assumed to be whole milk, eggs
and individual vegetables such as potatoes are medium, and pepper is
freshly ground black pepper.

The times given for each recipe are an approximate guide only because
the preparation times may differ according to the techniques used by
different people and the cooking times may vary as a result of the
type of oven used.

Recipes using raw or very lightly cooked eggs should be avoided by
infants, the elderly, pregnant women, convalescents and anyone
suffering from an illness.